A *Gloss on Our Painted Gods* is concerned with the idea of
translation: of poetry as translation, as a way of reinventing,
retelling, transforming and understanding the world around us,
our mythologies, our notions of the self and the other. It is
concerned with translation between languages, and also with
the translation of history, memory, emotion and experience –
that is, not *between* languages but simply *into* language. Each
poem in this collection, therefore, is a translation and, in some
cases, is a part of a larger schema of translation. What we
witness in each poem is a movement: from alphabet to alphabet,
from sign to sign.

A Gloss on Our Painted Gods
Eric Barstad

Frontenac House
Calgary, Alberta

Book design by EPIX Design Inc.
Author's portrait by Joslin Green.

National Library of Canada Cataloguing in Publication Data

Barstad, Eric.
  A gloss on our painted gods / Eric Barstad.

Poems.
ISBN 0-9732380-1-1

I. Title.
PS8553.A77G56 2003   C811'.6   C2003-910034-0
PR9199.4.B368G56 2003

Frontenac House gratefully acknowledges the support of Canada Council for the Arts and The Alberta Foundation for the Arts for our publishing program.

Printed and bound in Canada.
Published by Frontenac House Ltd.
1138 Frontenac Avenue S.W.
Calgary, Alberta, T2T 1B6, Canada
Tel: 403-245-2491   Fax: 403-245-2380
editor@frontenachouse.com   www.frontenachouse.com

1 2 3 4 5 6 7 8 9   07 06 05 04 03

For Mom and Dad
(and Errol)

For Erin

vos facitis, "ut spolium non sim, nec nuder ab illis,
naufragii tabulas qui petiere mei."
~ Ovid, *Tristia* 1.6.7-8

Acknowledgements

I'd like to thank everyone who helped in the crafting of these poems and in the crafting of this book as a whole: Ross Leckie; everyone in English 123: Poetry Workshop and at the Friday night meetings at the Ice House when I was still in Fredericton; John Ball, John Geyssen, and Anne Klinck; Anne Le Dressay and Paul Harland; David Dahle and Millo Shaw; Mom and Dad.

A number of these poems have appeared, or are forthcoming, in the following journals: *The Antigonish Review, Event, The Fiddlehead, Grain,* the *Harpweaver, Litwit Review, The Malahat Review, Pottersfield Portfolio, Prairie Fire, The Prairie Journal, Wascana Review,* and *Zygote.* Thank you to those editors who showed an interest in my work.

Contents

A Gloss on Our Painted Gods
  About the Poem I Wanted to Write 11
  The Half Movement of Stone 13
  The Last of the Wine 14
  Towards an Aviary 15
    i. Eagle 15
    ii. Peacock 16
    iii. Kingfisher 17
    iv. Magpie 18
    v. Osprey 19
    vi. Partridge 20
    vii. Hawk 21
  Icarus; or, The Start of Winter 22
  Echo's Lament (2) 23
  For Orpheus 24
  Arachne's Suitor, Years Later 25
  The Danaids 26
  The Six Labours of Theseus .27
  Achilles, famed sprinter, prays for his hands 31
  After the Sirens 32
  The Poetics of Loss 33
  Of an Oil Rome 36

Mythopoeia
  Gemma Tiberiana 39
  Vitam Impendere Vero 40
  Ascent 41
  Caligula De-lineated: Illness .42
  Caligula as the North Wind .43
  The Moon, or Happiness 44
  Swale 45
  On a Sister's Death 47
  On Discovering Caligula in a Video Store 48
  Sky Swims About Your Shoulders 49
  For Caligula 50
  Caligula and the Prairie Sky, After 52

An Etymology of Sorts
Pythagorean Love Triangle 55
Sin-Eater Self-Promotion 56
The Woodcutter's Son 57
The Misanthropy of Horizon 58
The Geologist to His Daughter .59
From St. Remy 60
Of Blood and Dandelions 61
Stigmata 62

An Ossuary of Lexical Shocks
Gypsy Ballad #3: Fight 65
Mercenary Songs 66
In a Time of War 67
Gospel 68
The Giantess 69
When Winter 70
In Genoa 71
In a Field, Walking 72
Gacela of the Unexpected Love .73
Echo's Lament 74
Hope Says 75
Threnody 76
Greek Love: A Prosopography of Loss 77
Recourse, a fragment 78

A Gloss on Our Painted Gods

"All old stories, my cousin,
will bear telling and telling again
in different ways."

~ Christabel LaMotte
in A.S. Byatt's *Possession*

About the Poem I Wanted to Write

I wanted to write a poem with epithets
and ancient Greek and Roman names.
I wanted to say pious, goddess-born Aeneas, or
Hector, tamer of horses.
                                    I wanted to allude
to obscure passages from long poems that nobody
reads anymore, unless to explain parts of other,
shorter, slightly less obscure poems.

Maybe I could have said something about dolphins –
I like dolphins – playing among the trees
of a flooded land. Or I could have written about
two senior citizens – too old for sex – throwing
their mother's bones behind them
in hopes of repopulating the world.

I would have mentioned Triton
– *Great God! I'd rather be a pagan* – wet beard
and all that, blowing his conch, summoning
who knows who from wherever.

                                    I would have put
Jupiter in my poem. Not the Jupiter – the swan,
the shower of gold, the mortal man – whose offspring
are legion and dalliances renowned, but the Jupiter
whose flowing locks shake the very foundations
of heaven and earth; the Jupiter who can give birth
from his head and thigh.

And I definitely would've talked about that blind prophet
who was a man then a woman then a man just because
he stepped on a snake, or killed a snake, or did something
to a snake.

But what I really wanted to do
was write a poem with Greek and Roman names,
and epithets, like pious, goddess-born Aeneas, and Hector,
tamer of horses.

The Half Movement of Stone
(Pyrrha & Deucalion)

"...these figures of men and their shapes
Will glisten again with motion..."
~ Wallace Stevens

The taste of dirt. Salt soil-caked to our lips.

The smell of dying fish.

And who, then, are these two, dry, veiled,
walking parallel, and parallel, tossing
– with the less-strength of age – our mother's
bones onto the ground, this ground filling
our mouths?

The sound of their soft slow steps
erases the thunder; their
synchronous steps: as love, as their love
used to be.
            Earlier days: his wrist
brushing her nipple in sleep, years
ago, before water's time. This
he thinks of now, osseous stones
– discarded like memories – dropping
behind him.

            Behind her: dust solidifying in time
with the falling rocks, the repetition sex-like,
but not. (Her palm against his chest.
A smoother palm, a harder chest.)

She smiles her grey smile,
glances at him and back at us: children,
our mouths still forming in the mud,
our dusty marrow.

The Last of the Wine

I still wonder how Ganymede managed
to convert the womanizing Jove, shift
the god's libido-gear, and cause him
to hold his breath. But, more and more,
I imagine how they would have parted,
Zeus and his cup-bearer.

An age-ridden god bent by the crook of years,
smelling of Ben Gay and chamomile tea,
eyes sunk into his wrinkled face, toga barely hanging
on his faded body.
                          And Ganymede. Maybe now
not so boyish, but splendid nonetheless, holding
the ancient, arthritic hands of Jupiter to his lips
for a final kiss. There would be an embrace that
even Hera would watch.

And Zeus would cry, smell secretly the boy
– now man – one last time as the others looked on.
Maybe Hephaestus, watching over Aphrodite's shoulder,
would know his next shield's design, the bellows
already blowing, the forges burning.

Towards an Aviary
(*After Ovid's* Metamorphoses)

i. Eagle
(*Aquila Rapax*)

With rare crepuscular exceptions, all
feed by day, none by night.

Yet a winged seize at twilight is this eagle's
whim and way, dusk-blue ground a sight

for sun-sore eyes. This is where we learn
the rapacity of lust's aviation; to bend

rules to the ocular curve of our own
desire. We bear thunder in our claws

and cannot forget: his back spasmed slick;
our head on her pulvinate breasts.

ii. Peacock
(Pavo Cristatus)

If these hundred eyes could close again,
what grey dream would they dream, so

exhausted by their own gaudy introspection?
Of a simple time, once, when the only

thing to watch was a bovine grazing, and
the meander of her threnodic low. Or, a story

heard, but not completed; a shepherd's slow
monotone; the quick cut of not waking.

iii. Kingfisher
(*Megaceryle alcyon*)

> *There is, however, a high*
> *mortality rate through drowning.*

Kingfisher flight is haunted,
haunting, like some lost limicoline

love returning lifeless in a dream,
water-filled and paler than memory.

Each dive is a shipwreck's full
potential, the chance of feathers

borne on surf to the shore, the etching
of dead names on empty tombs.

iv. Magpie
(*Pica pica*)

> *...and there they were,*
> *Magpies, the copses' saucy scolds.*

Their call is not cadence but complaint,
the cacophony of a contest lost. Their

call is a question of name, of what they've
become – *mag? mag?* – and affirmation.

They are the black bills that reach for tune
and come up short. They are nine times

unmusical and hold no hope for song, beauty
only in the green camber of their wings.

v. Osprey
(*Pandion haliaetus*)

> *...it hovers*
> *over a body of water and dives*
> *beneath the surface to capture*
> *fish in its talons.*

This is osprey as thurible, circling.
This is ritual, an effort to uncut

a father's purple tress; to take back
and bend the shears of filial

betrayal; to hate clearly and without
the meniscus blur of the sea's surface

distorting one's focus like tears. This
is fish as memory expunged, a kind

of cleansing, talons clutched, piercing,
as if in flesh, as if in one's own.

vi. Partridge
(*Perdix perdix*)

> *They prefer to run,*
> *and fly only short distances*

because they fear still the fall
that gave them wings and

their eponym. Witness how flight's
failure comes full circle: a nephew-

turned-bird at the compass centre,
a wax-winged son at the periphery.

Witness whose hands hold and
guide. Witness the compass drop.

vii. Hawk
(*Accipiter nisus*)

> *And now a hawk,*
> *Benign to none, he vents his savagery...*

We read of him here and only once,
trying to cauterize grief in a pyre's flames,

and failing. What burns: a daughter's body
and face; the tongue that first set the blaze

alight. Consolation comes in waves' white
noise on a stone shore, and as the cliff above.

We predict his leap and change, and the way
sorrow, like love, grows plumage too.

Icarus; or, The Start of Winter
(November: Fredericton, NB)

> "Winter lives under a pigeon's wing, a dead wing
> with damp feathers."
> ~ Elizabeth Bishop

Today, I find myself staring at this pigeon's wing
of winter, and the snow on the ground
is the diaphanous off-colour of a scar. Flakes

fall feather-thick from branches bent with the idea
of flight – that strain and hew for air, that altitudinal
longing. Here, trajectory turns into myth: a snowball's

arc and plummet like a wax-winged child's own;
a father's words – sun-altered and tremulous –
echoing at the cusp of hearing.

Echo's Lament (2)

"That false face fuels and
fools his delight…"

and mine. But I am marrow
and voice at a remove.

If I had hands, or breath
to blow, I would stir his liquid

likeness into indecipherable
rings and so release him.

Release him from the half-moon
in the half-moon of his eye. From

the blush he beats into his flesh.
From this eternal blossoming.

For Orpheus

Late summer and the red death of leaves.
He walks as if asleep and whispers to himself
a poem. About loss, of course, about death
and love. A typical poet? Yes,
and the first.

He fingers a scar on his chest
from love-making. He hasn't noticed
the birds, the trees, the rocks that have rolled
behind him. The insects humming
in time with him. Seven black bears
following like paparazzi. He hasn't
shielded his eyes from the sun
that hasn't moved.
                        Then he sits.
Looking around at the same clouds and trees
and birds as this morning, the seven black bears
and the flies that won't bite him, he imagines he's walked
in a circle, or worse, not at all. He believes this
is his new tragedy, dementia from loss and death,
and love.

So caught up in his next sorrow, he doesn't hear
the footfalls of women in the forest, the blood
sounding in their ears like a song.

Arachne's Suitor, Years Later

1.

I wake up and am standing
on my bed, trying to kill spiders
that are not there. This,
the third time in two nights.

The first night
I watch a spider descend upside-down
in moonlight, silver broken
by a thin spindle's eight legs.

Later, my eyes open to a silken star
seemingly inches away, though
lamplight reveals nothing
but sleep's eviction.

2.

Hate is what this is about.
What I hate: the knowledge that, when I'm asleep,
she could be spinning webs in my mouth, laying
her eggs in my ears.

Trespass is what this is about.
I mark my boundaries with her kin.
"This is the point of no return," I tell her.
"Outside I will not take your lives intentionally.
No one is innocent inside."

The Danaids

"The original impetus for this study sprang from the random discovery ... that the Danaid-water carriers, the thus far undisputed 'sinners in Hades', ... look incongruously happy."
~ Eva Keuls, *The Water Carriers in Hades*

To us, love is a lesser weight, a continual
leaking. In the sapphire spill, we provide

the ingredients for love's inevitable
loam: clay and rot, the scent of leaving

and recurrence. We are proof that forty-nine
ways to desire all lead to the selfsame thrust

and immolation, the motile pairing of blade
and body where blood becomes a language

that speaks itself dry on sheets and skin.
If only all such punishments were as sweet:

a gradual emptying, and the arms' lesser ache.

The Six Labours of Theseus

1.

> ... *his mother Aethra,* ... *informing him who his true father*
> *was, commanded him to take from thence the tokens that*
> *Aegeus had left, and sail to Athens* ..., *but he refused to take*
> *his journey by sea, though it was much the safer way.*

Alone, Theseus imagines his mother,
her chemise raised waist-high by the ocean's
stalwart finger – how, in love's aftermath, silt
was a tegument that must have left a trail
down the inside of her thigh: a portent
of his birth.
            But now, from this cliff, the sea
seems frenetic; Theseus sees not open arms
but unwelcome
               signs that say, *Hit the road.*

So, when Corynetes ("club-bearer")
blocks his path, Theseus grins
hate, steals the weapon, and beats death
in bruises down the other man's back.

The club he keeps as a killer's trophy,
like fingernails or a lock of hair.

2

Sinis, a thief and bender of trees,
pine sap on his palms. In this story,
the fight's not worth describing
but for the end: Theseus tying Sinis's
wrists to one bowed pine, his ankles
to another: trees straightening, the sound
of tearing sinew.

As if that weren't enough, Theseus
woos Sinis's daughter, splits her
in a different way. She sprouts a son, and he
(years later) breeds a litter of peaceful
green children.

3.

> The Crommyonian sow, which they called Phaea, was a
> savage and formidable wild beast, by no means an enemy to
> be despised. ... Others relate that Phaea was a woman.

Because eating is noble and bacon is good,
he chases Phaea, Sow of Crommyon,
with a lust for salted meat.

But in the silence of the kill's completion,
the first fissures appear: those riffs in language
like rent flesh; how creophagy

changes shape and remoulds the tongue's
desire. How do we reconcile that other
taste; how suture our disconsolate hunger?

4

Sciron was accustomed, out of insolence and wantonness, to
stretch forth his feet to strangers commanding them to wash
them, and then while they did it, with a kick, sent them down
the rock into the sea.

On a red-figure *kylix*, Sciron
pleads for his life, already
falling, the giant turtle waiting below.

If this cup were half-filled with water,
the effect would be marvellous: the turtle
submerged, Sciron himself beginning

to sink, and Theseus standing on the cliff,
his right leg raised, his feet newly clean,
his arms lifted in celebration.

5

Fighting those ready for a fight
is always the hardest, thinks Theseus, staring
at Cercyon, this André-the-Giant of a man
who's come dressed in lion-skin
and is missing no teeth.

What we don't see: half-nelson, full-
nelson, lariat, a cover, a two-count, repeat. Off
the ropes, over the ropes, bound and gagged
with ropes, steel chair. Steel chair.

What we do: Theseus with Cercyon high
over his head, bloodied and bedraggled, beaten.
Theseus with Cercyon high over his head,
dashing him down and jagged on rocks.

6

In Procrustes' B&B severed feet are doily-topped
and tied with crimped ribbon; the one bed
has a crimson quilt and teeth placed like mints
on the fluffed pillows.
                        Still, Theseus signs in
(though not his real name) and sizes up his bed
for sleep. Procrustes – ever mindful of his guest's
comfort – comes to tuck Theseus in
with an axe and a rack made for stretching.

Now, it's not clear how Procrustes ends up
in the bed, his feet dangling over the baseboard,
Theseus with the axe and a tape measure.
After an initial intestinal shriek, Procrustes passes out,
and Theseus (not even done with the left leg)
pulls a blanket to the floor and goes to sleep.

Achilles, famed sprinter, prays for his hands

in shade, where he is shade, where Styx and Acheron
haemorrhage over their banks. As part of the roll call
of the dead, he salutes without hands, and where once
were hands is a mocking of flesh, ravens setting to flight,
darkness feathered.

Once, Odysseus entered this place like a demon from
above, still solid, hands held out to Achilles, and told
of Penelope's weaving, of her years on the loom, of her
tearing and repairing of thread. And had there been a sky,
it would have turned dark and fat with February – clouds
like whales coming to shore.

After the Sirens

"A roaring voice, hoarse with salted longing."
~ Shane Rhodes

After the Sirens, we
ask him of their song and
he tells us nothing, wiping
the wet from his eyes.
Our ears stopped with wax, we
heard only the sea as if underwater
and watched him struggle
against the ropes, blood
redding his wrists.

We imagine
they sang – with a single
voice – some song full
of salted longing, tentacle
notes tempting him
ashore. But he offers us
none of this, stares
from the prow,
aimed forward, aimed
homeward, humming
beneath his breath.

The Poetics of Loss

i.

"I will not
detain you or dispute your story."

Leaving is the febrifuge of all
desire, the flattening of the voice's

tensile melody. We are all abandoned
eventually and learn to withhold

the interrogatives of going and
of being left. Thus Dido, once

lachrymose, turned ferric and sharp,
her body the blade that hewed

the hawser and set the ships to sea.

ii.

Aeneas, now quite certain
of departure, took the boon of sleep.

A kind of indolence, this. The emotional
sort where one – weary from coital

exhumation – simply gives in, shuts his eyes
to everything but the future. Yet

even in sleep, he can find no rest,
for his dreams take the shape of a god's

resolve: to move on, to ignore his name
as it's called from the shore – this

is the only way out. Look skyward.
Pretend it is the stars that guide him now.

iii.

"Let the cold Trojan,
far at sea, drink in this conflagration."

What thin script is this that presses
itself upon the iron sky, solemn

and bereft? We try to cull words
from its coiling, guess its author's

carpal bend. The Captain seems
sick, febrile from the sight of the sky's

epistle, and he cuts a straighter course
from the Carthaginian shore, intense

as man who swallows flames and
can never quite shake the taste of ash.

Of an Oil Rome

> "Then banish'd Faith shall once again return,
> And Vestal fires in hallow'd temples burn;
> And Remus with Quirinus shall sustain
> The righteous laws, and fraud and force restrain."
> ~ Jupiter prophesying the return of the Golden Age

In the painted sleep of fig trees, leaves
float in silence, and prophecy lurches

like old age. The wind stands still
around the brushed echoes of tree tops;

the oil sky is encased, is a whisper of
peach and mauve. In the distance, a

mountain juts out from a lip of pines
and bites the disappearing sun. A river

in the corner reflects six birds blackened
by the fading light – six birds whose omen

owns these crumbled pillars from this
crumbled past.

Mythopoeia

"... unless they are very carefully handled, facts
are the invariable tyrants of story."

~ Rudy Wiebe

Gemma Tiberiana

"The first-century Grand Cameo of Paris or 'Gemma
Tiberiana,' possibly showing Tiberius receiving Germanicus
on his return from the Rhine, or giving him his commission
before his journey to the East. The figures behind
Germanicus on the far left could be Agrippina and the five-
year-old Caligula."
                    ~ Arther Ferrill, *Caligula: Emperor of Rome*

This is ivory childhood rimmed in gold, my thumb
as big as your body. You are a boy in battle gear,
five years old, leaning against your mother's leg,
your father before his emperor-brother, gods like clouds

in the sky. Five years old and already you know
death's iron on iron, the fetor of flesh rotting and burnt.
Years later, you will hold your mother's ashes
and think of this moment. You will enter Rome

as she must have with the ashes of your poisoned father.
But now you are cut and carved into the relief
of this cameo's world, resting against your mother's
thigh, the scent of death nowhere around you.

Vitam Impendere Vero

I will not starve here in the umber
of cold Caesar's shadow, enveloped
in avuncular disrepute. I will not starve,
for I am fat from my grandmother's
callous designs: the way she let her own
daughter die and never offered up a scrap
of remorse.
          My brother and mother
starved and I will not. My brother, in jail,
stranger to light and food, found survival
in his mattress's coarse and grainy fill
till his stomach was no longer fooled.
My mother, an exile, believed poison
on the tip of every tine, and she died
not from ingestion, but from what
she could not swallow.

But I, uncle, emperor, I will not starve.
I will bend my back and walk a softer path;
I will kiss your hands and learn to acquiesce;
I will feast and pick my teeth with bones.

Ascent
(*March 16, 37 AD*)

Late afternoon and sunlight
trails the ground like a cape.
We are a parade of death following
the leak of our shadows home.

It occurs to me now that
there is no more remollient weapon
than suffocation: to force one
to seek air where air is not, where breath
is not, where a pillow's pressure slows
the pulse to an inevitable stillness.

Death is a gift one cannot
take back, and it would seem
I am generous to a fault.

Caligula De-lineated: Illness
(Autumn, 37 AD)

> "Why did I come to it? Where is it drawn?
> How does it lie, and what divide?
> If I speak of blood, will you not admit
> that selfsame pattern holds you up?"
> ~ Tim Bowling, "The Line"

i.

"Brain fever" and the sea's
in my ears, the urge of waves, that certain
erosion that shifts the sand, gnawing.
I have forgotten the month now
and they keep the sunlight from my eyes.

ii.

The veins in my arm seem arboreal,
rooted in the earth of my heart, my dirt
heart. So will you not admit? Will you not?

iii.

There are sleepers in the streets,
and all the night is gravid with dreams
of health. Philanthropic tokens have touched
the air, stellar in the ovoid darkness.
But I am long past the veridical, homing in now
on consequence, and I am sure this will become
strophe, Suetonian segue: "So much
for the prince, and now..."
                                        I am well.

Caligula as the North Wind

"By force I drive
The weeping clouds, by force I whip the sea,
Send gnarled oaks crashing, pack the drifts of snow,
And hurl the hailstones down upon the lands."
~ Boreas (*Metamorphoses* 6.680-683)

The trees bleed summer from their leaves
and he is Boreas, his teeth like ice, blizzards
in his eyes. He echoes in our ears, freezes us
with a tongue of frost.

These are days of myth and blasphemy.

In a gust, he lines ships across the Bay
of Naples, pulls the sun into darkness
to white the night sky, leaving us a people
without food.
                 He takes wives like Zeus,
leaves them cold and hollowed out, debauched
by a breeze.
                 Pneumonia is the hand
he plunges into the wet lung of the city,
and our sudden decline: the way the land
acquiesces to winter and grows colourless
as a corpse.

The Moon, or Happiness

"Really, this world of ours, the scheme of things as they call
it, is quite intolerable. That's why I want the moon, or
happiness, or eternal life – something, in fact, that may
sound crazy, but which isn't of this world."
                    ~ Caligula in Albert Camus's *Caligula*

Perhaps you thought of each as light
to land on, never once imagining the rills
and craters, the pocks of closer inspection.
Perhaps you believed each was the other's
equal, the moon and happiness, a smile
and its effigy.
                    Yet, like all else, this
is conjecture; you are silent, silent as I am now
in the sullen static of rain against the window
of my no-bedroom apartment.

Would you still strain for the moon, this moon
hidden by poplar leaves, hidden by a pedestrian
bridge and a cold night's cumulus, hidden as always,
an impossibility, one of those fallacies of sight, the sun's
mineral reflection, a reminder of what is always
out of reach?

Swale

"Of his sisters, Caligula is believed to have spoiled the
virgin Drusilla when he was just a boy... The rest of his
sisters he did not love with so great affection."
~ Suetonius

i.

Your breathing is the only movement
in this stillness, and I am held
by the pull of your sleep.

In the closet of your eyes, you mouth
soft words I can hardly decipher: songs
that drop in beads from the edge
of your tongue and land in my palm.

You laugh, singing me
into your dream.

ii.

You've almost disappeared, but
let me lie beside you where shadows
swallow us. Pressed to your back, I
run my hand over your frailty: ribs
barely beneath the skin, this hollow
at your waist.
                    We know home
in this darkness. Your eyes are closed
and you smile (once again in childhood),
calling me Little Boots. Outside,
trees wave through the night.

iii.

I dreamt myself old,
slender, and grey-haired.
A woman clothed in white,
old like me, took me
in her arms, soft hands.

I thought it was you.

On a Sister's Death
(*June 10, 38 AD*)

"The sea is a woman's body I have lost."
~ Richard Taylor, *Tender Only to One*

Heat waves the air. You are as if
underwater; you are liquid in the thick

of day, going westward, going seaward
into our initial element, our sea-shine azure

womb. I watch you from this cave
of dreams, dissolved pearl speech drifting white

from your lips – hungry love. I float to you,
my body brushing this humid weight of curled air

and stopped breath. You etch your name
in sandstone, then mine, and "Soon," you say,

"soon enough." You begin to fade, a falling
nocturne, a denouement, and are gone.

I run my fingers through your absence.

On Discovering Caligula in a Video Store

So this is what you have become.

Though I have looked for you in histories
whose authors were too offended to pen

even your name, as if scalded by the roll and flow
of its script, and in novels where you burst from the womb

a killer, murder engraved on your bones, I find you
on this box where the profile on the cover's coin

is not your own, but an actor's square, side-
long glance. "Malcolm McDowell *is*

Caligula." Who, then, are you? Hollywood's
early Roman bad boy, pornography's

precursor. And who – since I have sunk my heels
in the blood-syntax of your past and fingered the bronze

currency of your grief – does that make me?

Sky Swims About Your Shoulders

> "Eleazar, the Parthian hostage, who was ... over eleven foot high. ... Caligula had [Eleazar's] body stuffed and dressed in armour and put Eleazar outside the door of his bed-chamber to frighten away would-be assassins."
> ~ Robert Graves, *I, Claudius*

Eleazar, I feel night like an avalanche,
and each morning I dust rubble
from my brow. I am weak
from the weight of it.

While walking in the gardens, I noticed the gladioli
are finally up, but they have the look of soothsayers, prophecy
on their stamen-tongues. I feel winter's quiet call
in their twisting leaves, a sombre funeral in snow.

And the chalice-bottom moon, Eleazar,
is so far away.
                    No, not for you – you
are two men tall, sky swims about
your shoulders, and you are eye
to eye with that resplendent, orbed
goddess, her voice like stars. But your armour
has lost its shine. Just look how old
I seem, reflected there. We have not,
I think, aged well.

For Caligula

Late January, the sky soft, hushed
with cloud, silent as the hostages your German guards take
at the news of your murder. They hold an entire arena captive
and sing to their spears.
                    Loyalty this, this act
of vengeance, this ability to reciprocate death with death,
to kill statistically: a single crowd's annihilation for that
of a single emperor. A wonderful simplicity.

        *

I stand, now, ankle-deep in the blood omen
of your death, frozen by marble laughter.
Frozen, too, by the sight of you falling earthward,
divinity sloughing from your body
like troubled sleep.

        *

In the Lamian Gardens where you were buried,
I fill my pockets with soil that stains my fingers black,
the wind off the Tiber comforting me as I mourn your death
despite everything.

        *

I watched (watch still) as your wife, grief-bent
over your body, could not speak her sorrow and
was stabbed, your two-year-old daughter
hoisted by her ankles, swung like a staff, her head
collapsing into a wall.

                And you, I saw, run through
for each year of your life, losing half your jaw
to someone's iron blade, your right eye. Before
you were dead, they castrated you and ate pieces
of your flesh.

I imagine kneeling next to you in the carnage's
respite, after each palm and sword had been wiped
immaculate, and listening to the queries of your breath.
I followed you because you made me laugh –
your raid on Neptune, soldiers gathering seashells
as booty; Incitatus, your horse, set up in a mansion
of his own, then made a senator, then
a High Priest of your temple.

But even now I want something in return:
acknowledgement – a faint nod telling me
that you are looking forward
and see me with my hand stretched out
as I lead you from the darkness, from this Palatine
underworld of the past; or, a whisper:
Don't look back; never look back.

Caligula and the Prairie Sky, After
(Fredericton, NB)

Tonight, after everything, he's become
a reminder of trains incising the darkness, all
window-rattle and hum at 2:00 a.m.

But this is not what I want, Caligula
and the prairie sky entwined, one
as the other's metonym. Surely this began

as a reaching homeward, a grasp
for thinner air, for wheatfields,
of course, and how here no trains

make us prescient of their coming;
no trains set the spark that sets the grass
along the tracks aflame, a flame

always unaware its lucency's the very thing
that blacks the ash and clears us out
like memory. So it is that I remember

fallowed fields and their endless stitch
of track; or the Rockies, a kind of
afterthought, overlooked until they're

out of sight; so it is that Caligula,
unrequested, becomes the prairie sky –
the very mingling of my memories –

growing dark, already dark, with gravel-
dust and smoke; growing dark, already dark,
with Mountain time.

An Etymology of Sorts

"There is a perfect rout of characters in every man
– and every man is like an actor's trunk,
full of strange creatures new and old."
~ Wallace Stevens

Pythagorean Love Triangle
(A letter, 556 BC)

Darling, you are the point at which
he and I converge, loving at right angles.
You should know he is all sepal
and selvage, those subtler prisons
that prevent unravelling. And while I seem
exactitude's self, the sum of insouciant sides,
I am, in fact, an unexpected bend, part
of a pterygoid whole that blades the air
in your direction. He can offer you
the exonumia of desire, but what
of love's calcareous corpse when
you both grow tired of your initial, tangling
geometry? What blood, then, will fill
the apertures of your serrulate heart;
whose theorem solve its beating riddle?

Sin-Eater Self-Promotion

For future reference, I would like
you to know that, for a small
gratuity, I can make your heaven-bound
voyage a light and less lengthy one.
All I need is for you to tear and place
a piece of bread upon your dead
loved one's chest, and I will – for
a mere pittance – take it, this newly
leavened sin, upon myself.
                              It's funny,
isn't it, how transgression and redemption
take on a similar edible form (though
the former, I'll admit, comes from a grander,
more delectable loaf).

No excessive piece need be laid down
for excessive sin – one slice fits all,
from the murderer to the drunkard, from
the pithless pontificate to the very hero
of hedonism. But – and I can't stress this
enough – the bread must be fresh: I'd hate
for your husbands and sons, wives and
daughters, to be hell-sent on account of stale,
spavined bread.

There's no need to disclose
your sins – bury them in their baking;
cipher them away in the concavities
of kneaded dough – for they all
taste the same to me.

The Woodcutter's Son

The river is high and I follow
its gelid, yellow flow; follow
the effluvium of mud. It is
that penumbral part of day
when light and dark are joined
in a kind of feral concupiscence,
and the sibilant wind,
and the luffing of leaves.

In the distance, the monosyllabic hacks
of my father's language: so empty
of Latinate phrases.

The Misanthropy of Horizon
(In search of Coppermine River, Canada, 1770)

Hunger's hurt has taken us far beyond tolerance
for Hearne's bravado. The Indians
have started to eat at the skin of their garments,

buck long-since dead and ragged with wear.
It's been six days since I've been able to shit,
chewing on leather. There is no shelter here

in the flats, and we've torn up the tent for shoes;
the only fire comes from moss we gather in palmfuls,
sifting through the scalloped snow, the sun

turning its back on us, the drunken wind
blowing in circles. This is the misanthropy of horizon:
to never see the line between grey and white broken

by animal or bird or the welcome philosophy of trees.
And yet, it is some greater malignance that desires us now,
and we hear it in the lake's low growl beneath the ice.

The Geologist to His Daughter

"Gutta cavat lapidem, non vi, sed saepe cadendo."
(The water droplet hollows out a stone, not by force,
but by dripping often.)
~ Ovid, *Ex Ponto*

This rock, so smooth and round
you place it in your mouth. At

my incomprehension-laugh,
Like glass, you say, *like*

a marble, as if this answer
could explain it all, could make me understand

how glass and marble somehow equal
the need to taste, to search with your tongue

the years of erosion that sit, silent,
on this one stone, its stiffened veins

reminders of the years – the winds and water
that all seem to flow the one same way.

I search for a word to describe
this movement: *cadere*, Latin,

to flow, to fall, but more than that –
a description of life, liquid, and air

simultaneously, a description rolling
smooth as glass, as weathered stone,

on my tongue. I want to offer you this,
this one spherical verb, my understanding,

but you stop me, spitting years,
sediment into my palm.

From St. Remy

"I could not paint this room. The chair says nothing to me,
the bed remains a bed."
~ Van Gogh, in Richard Taylor's *Tender Only to One*

I sit alone in frost-white rooms
and tie paper into knots. There is

swirled sunshine in each knot, grass
in each virgin page. There is no ceremony

in my discarding, just paper falling
into piles near my shoeless feet.

Of Blood and Dandelions

When I was a boy, my
father greeted strangers with
tobacco-spit and curse-filled
laughter. *Hard* and *Work* were
the words that ran the rills of his face
like sweat. He dug ditches. Soil
was the colour of his skin.
He died without exclamation.

Mother was thin from love and
love's produce. She had dusty
eyes and raised us – 13 of us –
as if we mattered. We didn't
starve, but nine turned out
to be a better number.

In the summers, my sisters
and I picked dandelions for tea.
I helped them because I was too small
to work on my brother's farm.
Often, we'd stay out for hours, seeing
no one but our shadows, and
we liked it that way.

My brother, though he farmed, loved
the trees, and the year he died there was no sky –
trees stood in paused explosion
and hid blue from us. We buried him
behind our house where he could grow roots
like the trees he loved.

And now, alone, I no longer drink
dandelion tea. I have inherited
this memory of yellow weeds, these hands
as hard and dark as dirt, my dusty eyes.

Stigmata

You sit cross-legged
writing in blue
on cigarette packs
and table cloths
and brown paper bags

You encrypt your tales
of Beer-Bottle Daddy
Deaf-Mute Mommy
trying to forget burns and words

> *My heart is an owl*
> *that sings at night*
> *without any feathers*

You've been pinned to the rug
no rescue anywhere
just impaling and praying
and dreams crawling from your head

> *My body knows*
> *the trombone between your thighs*
> *and is tired of your music*

Now
there are dapples of blood
like confession
beside you in the tub
cloudy water forgiving you
though getting colder

> *Pennies ripple water wishless*

and bodies get tired of flinching

An Ossuary of Lexical Shocks

"Matisse says somewhere that a reproduction
requires as much talent for color as the original
painting. I have been tormented by the fraudulence
of my own heavy touch."
~ Robert Lowell

Gypsy Ballad #3: Fight
(Federico García Lorca, "Reyerta")

Halfway down the hill we see the blades
of the Albacete, beautiful with blood and
glinting like fish. From the sky's acrid green,
tarot-hard light cuts the silhouettes
of maddened horses and their riders.
There are two old women weeping
atop an olive tree and a bull building barricades
to protect himself.

> *And dark angels supply kerchiefs and melted*
> *snow, angels with wings like Albacete blades.*

Beside me, Juan Antonio rolls dead down the slope,
his body full of lilies, and a pomegranate
in his head – Juan Antonio riding a cross of fire
along the highway of the dead. Along
the ground, trickling blood groans
a muted serpent song, and the afternoon – crazed
with figtrees and the buzz of heat – falls unconscious
across the thighs of wounded riders.

> *And dark angels cut through the air,*
> *angels with tresses and olive hearts.*

Mercenary Songs
(*Archilochos*)

i.

Some Saian exults in my shield – blameless
battle gear – which I left near a bush
in my retreat. But I preserved myself
from danger, so what do I care?
I will find another just as good.

ii.

A thousand killers.
Seven dead.

iii.

Corpses in moonlight, eaten
by Sirius.

iv.

Let the young rush into battle;
victory is god-granted, and Ares
is a democrat.

v.

As one in thirst desires drink,
so I to do battle with you.

vi.

The way one cuts skin
from the back of the neck.
The way we, in the hospitality
of war, left them their dead
to remember us by.

In a Time of War
(Giuseppe Ungaretti, "I fiumi")

Tonight, leaning against the scars
of this tree, abandoned in a river valley
that has the languor of a circus
before the show, I watch the nomadic
clouds cross the country of the moon.

This morning, I stretched myself out
in the water's tepid urn and lay
like a relic, the Isonzo polishing me
like one of its stones.

Yet, there have been times
when I've pulled myself together
and sprung like an acrobat across
the water; when I have knelt
next to my war-filthy clothes
and, like a Bedouin, bent my head
to receive the sun.

Gospel
(Antonio Machado, *"Tal vez la mano, en sueños"*)

Perhaps that dreaming hand
that first sowed the stars
sounded too a forgotten music

like a note from a huge and ancient lyre
and the humble wave that came to our lips
came as a few honest words.

The Giantess
(Charles Baudelaire, "La Géante")

If the earth were still gravid with all
her monstrous children, I would want to live
near a young giantess
like a cat at the feet of a queen.

I'd love to watch her soul's body blossom
and grow freely in her terrible play; to see
if her heart might hatch a sombre flame,
or mists which would swim in her eyes. I'd love,

in my leisure, to traverse her splendid shape,
clamber sidelong up the slope of her knees, and
surely, some summer day, when the sun

had laid her out across the countryside, sleep
nonchalantly in the shade of her breasts
like a peaceful town at the mountain's foot.

When Winter
(Horace, Odes, 1.9)

Because the Soracte is bleached with snow, trees
stooped with the white weight of it, and the rivers
still, I pray for the retreat of cold, hang firelight
on the wall with a hook, draw wine from a Sabine jug,
and the Spring. Letting the gods pay the tab, I toast
the unknown, the future, the future I do not care
to know, wanting to love and dance while I can.

I walk the field of summer memories with the whispers
of lovers soft in the clear pitch of night. But these
are overcome by a woman's laughter in this room's
dark corner where we sit, where she feigns
to stop me as I remove her bracelets and rings.

In Genoa
(Dino Campana, "Donna genovese")

You come for me with bits of seaweed
still in your hair and this sirocco's scent –
all ardour and distance-weak – which falls
the length of your body: not as love,
but as the ghost of that longing
which wanders – serene and inescapable –
the pilgrimage of one's heart, and dissolves.

So will you show me what the wind
can bear on its back; how small the world,
the light, can seem in your hands?

In a Field, Walking
(Antonio Machado, "Campo")

The afternoon is dying,
a humble hearth that puts itself

out. Over the mountains, a
few hot coals remain. Always,

there is that broken tree on the
white road, only two

branches on its wounded
trunk, and a leaf, faded and

black, on each branch. Are
you crying? Among the

golden poplars, the shadow of
love waits for you.

Gacela of the Unexpected Love
(Federico García Lorca, "Gacela del Amor Imprevisto")

No one understood the magnolia scent
of your belly. No one knew you martyred
love's hummingbird between your teeth, or that
Persian horses slept in the plaza beneath the moon
of your forehead, or that for four nights
I held your waist, enemy of the snow.

Now, between gypsum and jasmine, your look
is a pale shoot of seeds, and I search my chest
for the ivory letters that say *always, always,
always.* Your body – the garden of my agony –
will always be a fugitive, your blood in my mouth,
your mouth dark with my going.

Echo's Lament
(Anonymous, "Levis exsurgit zephirus")

"... Touch my lips, and so unseal them;
I have learned silence since I lived and died."
~ Marjorie Pickthall

These breezes from the west. The honey sun sliding
across the arched back of the world. Lilacs and maples

in bloom. Squirrels in the half-dream of spring –
somnambulists waking to the tune of bird-song,

to the building of nests and homes of their own. All this,
and I alone, pale with my reflections, these thoughts

that open like petals, "ashen and sere and grey."
I am a new kind of quiet, and I desire –

I desire you, that you might know this verdant rerun;
that you might witness my slow escape, my silent departure.

Hope Says
(Antonio Machado, "Dice la esperanza")

Hope says: one day
you will see her, if
you can learn to wait.

Despair says: she is
your bitterness. Beat,
heart. The world has not
swallowed everything.

Threnody
(Ovid, Tristia 1.4)

We cleave this azurite Ionian ocean against our wills.
Star-stirred by constellations, winds swell the sea, lift wave
upon wave over this prow and stern, strip the gloss

from our painted gods. These pine planks echo the pulse and pull
of the water's heart, ropes sound their strain, and I know the
    confession
in the captain's pallor: he is a charioteer who – too weak – has
    let drop

the reins upon his obdurate horse's neck; we go
where the sea wants, our rider having surrendered the sail
to the ship. And we will not reach that place approached

unless Aeolus lets loose his changing winds: we've left
the Illyrian shores far behind, and Italy – forbidden – is now all
I can see. I pray, wind, obey with me this emperor's blade

at my back; for what's left but prayer? What's left
but to follow some blue god from this wet sepulchre and
be led from death, already dead?

Greek Love: A Prosopography of Loss
(Diodorus Zonas)

Charon – you who bend death's
boat through these pools of reeds

and murk – stretch out your dark
hands to my son as he climbs

from the hull: look
how he slips in his sandals,

and he is afraid to set
his barefoot prints upon the shore.

Recourse, a fragment
(*Catullus, 14a*)

If, by chance, you should
come upon these poems and
still want to touch me
with your hands...

Notes on the Poems

The epigraph to the section "A Gloss on Our Painted Gods" comes from A.S. Byatt's *Possession* (Random House, 1990).

The epigraph to "The Half Movement of Stone" is from "Sad Strains of a Gay Waltz", *The Collected Poems of Wallace Stevens* (Vintage, 1990).

The italicized lines that begin sections i and iii of "Towards an Aviary" is from *Birds: Their Life, Their Ways, Their World* (Reader's Digest Association, 1979). Those which begin sections v and vi are used with permission from Microsoft Corporation as made available through Microsoft® Encarta® Encyclopedia 2000. Those in sections iv and vii come from Ovid's *Metamorphoses* translated by A.D. Melville (Oxford University Press, 1986), as are the italicized lines that begin "Echo's Lament (2)", and "Caligula as the North Wind"

The epigraph to "Icarus; or, The Start of Winter" comes from Elizabeth Bishop's "Paris, 7 a.m." published in *Elizabeth Bishop: The Complete Poems 1927-1979* (Farrar, Straus and Giroux, 1999).

Epigraphs in "The Six Labours of Theseus" are from Plutarch's *Life of Theseus*.

The epigraph to "After the Sirens" is from Shane Rhodes' poem "Clytaemnestra" published in *The Wireless Room* (NeWest Press, 2000).

The italicized lines that open the three poems in "The Poetics of Loss" all come from Virgil's *Aeneid* translated by Robert Fitzgerald (Vintage, 1990).

The epigraph to "Of an Oil Rome" is from Dryden's translation of the *Aeneid*.

The quotation that begins the section "Mythopoeia" comes from Rudy Wiebe's essay "On the Trail of Big Bear" published in *A Voice in the Land: Essays By and About Rudy Wiebe* edited by W.J. Keith (NeWest Press, 1981).

The epigraph to "Gemma Tiberiana" comes from Arther Ferrill's *Caligula: Emperor of Rome* (Thames and Hudson, 1991).

The epigraph to "Caligula De-lineated: Illness" is from Tim Bowling's "The Line" in *The Thin Smoke of the Heart* (McGill-Queen's University Press, 2000).

The epigraph to "The Moon, or Happiness" comes from Albert Camus' *Caligula and Three Other Plays* (Knopf, 1958).

The epigraph to "Swale" comes from Suetonius' *The Lives of the Caesars*.

The epigraphs to "On a Sister's Death" and to "From St. Remy" come from Richard Taylor's *Tender Only to One* (Oberon Press, 1984).

The epigraph to "Sky Swims About Your Shoulders" comes from Robert Graves' *I, Claudius* (Arthur Barker, 1934).

"The Misanthropy of Horizon" is based loosely on parts of Samuel Hearne's *A Journey from Prince of Wales Fort*.

The quotation that introduces the section "An Ossuary of Lexical Shocks" comes from Robert Lowell's essay "On Imitations" published in *Collected Prose* edited by Robert Giroux (Farrar, Straus and Giroux, 1987).

"In a Time of War" is loosely based on Giuseppe Ungaretti's "I fiumi" in *The Penguin Book of Italian Verse* edited by George Kay (Penguin, 1960).

The epigraph to "Echo's Lament" is from Marjory Pickthall's "Resurgam." The quotation within the poem is from D.C. Scott's "The Sea by the Wood."

Originally from a small Alberta farming community east of Calgary, Eric Barstad currently lives and writes in Camrose, Alberta, where he teaches English Literature and Creative writing at Augustana University College and moonlights as a legal assistant. He completed his MA in English and Creative writing at the University of New Brunswick in 2001. *A Gloss on our Painted Gods* is his first book.